CHICAGO
MARATHON

FRONT COVER: In the early stages of the 2008 race, these runners illustrate the spirit, drive, and determination of the nearly 40,000 athletes who compete in the Chicago Marathon each year. (Courtesy Raymond Britt.)

BACK COVER: Nearly a century earlier, a group of runners stood at the starting line in Grant Park, to begin one of Chicago's first marathons. (Courtesy Chicago History Museum.)

COVER BACKGROUND: Runners take the exciting first strides to begin an extraordinary 26.2 mile journey at the 2007 Chicago Marathon. (Courtesy Raymond Britt.)

CHICAGO
MARATHON

Raymond Britt

ARCADIA
PUBLISHING

Published by Arcadia Publishing
Charleston SC, Chicago IL, Portsmouth NH, San Francisco CA

Printed in the United States of America

Library of Congress Control Number: 2009928806

For all general information contact Arcadia Publishing at:
Telephone 843-853-2070
Fax 843-853-0044
E-mail sales@arcadiapublishing.com
For customer service and orders:
Toll-Free 1-888-313-2665

Visit us on the Internet at www.arcadiapublishing.com

For Wendy, Amanda, Rebecca, Eric and Kirsten

CONTENTS

ACKNOWLEDGMENTS

The world of endurance events is filled with generous people, communities, and institutions joining together in the spirit of swimming, biking, running, coaching, advising, writing, and more. This book wouldn't be possible without a wide spectrum of people both on the course and off of it who joined me for the journey to the finish line and beyond. I thank you one and all for the exceptional experiences we've shared so far.

I wish to thank my team at Arcadia Publishing, led by Jeff Ruetsche for expert guidance and teamwork. I also wish to thank my Arcadia proofreader, Sara Desharnais. All classic-era images in this book are from the Chicago Daily News negatives collection, courtesy of Chicago History Museum. Historical content benefited from archives at the Chicago History Museum, the New York Times, the Chicago Tribune, and others. Present day race statistics and perspectives were gleaned from a wide variety of local and national print, web, and running-specific media sources.

All modern era photographs and direct race commentary are mine, from personal experience inside and outside the race, while running the Chicago Marathon 12 times since 1994.

INTRODUCTION

The runners anxiously awaited the signal to start the race. Each carried a personal reason for being there; each envisioned what lay ahead at the finish line. Unsure of exactly what would happen between the start and finish, they knew this: in the marathon anything can happen.

They also knew that the marathon they were about to begin was of world-class caliber, with significant city, corporate, and community support and involvement. It was organized to be the world's best marathon, with no expense spared, no detail left unchecked.

The marathon course was flat and fast, encouraging hope that a new world record would be set by an elite runner. The route would take runners through a showcase of the city of Chicago's proud and diverse neighborhoods including Grant Park, Lincoln Park, and the South Side. As many as 10 percent of the city's population would line the streets to cheer. It was a marathon runner's dream.

It was just like the world-class marathon the city and runners have come to expect year after year in Chicago. Except this one was different.

It was September 23, 1905. This race was the first Chicago Marathon.

In early 1905, the newly formed Illinois Athletic Club made a bold decision: Chicago would set the world standard for the marathon in terms of size, support, ethics, and athleticism. The marathon would epitomize everything that Chicago and its citizens represented: character, strength, spirit.

At 2:00 p.m. on that late September day, 15 determined runners bolted at the sound of the starter's gun to begin an amazing journey of distance and endurance. Huge crowds witnessed a thrilling race that had it all, including action, disaster, suspense, a fallen favorite, and a cliffhanger ending. It was epic, defining a new chapter in Chicago's athletic history.

In years to come, the marathon would continue to capture the imagination of Chicago with exciting races and unpredictable outcomes. After the 1907 marathon, the *Chicago Tribune* led with this headline: "Sleeping Runner Loses Marathon; Lindquist Trots Two Miles as Somnambulist; Collapses a Mile from Goal." Two years later, the post-race headline read: "Boy Outrace 71 in I.A.C. Chicago Marathon" as teenager L. J. Pillivant stunned runners, experts, and spectators alike. Year after year, the city and communities rallied around the marathon as one of the most extraordinary events in the nation.

More than 100 years later, the race has become one of the largest and most popular marathons in the world, a race where elites come to break world records, and where first-time runners simply race to become a marathon finisher.

And now, every October, Chicago is home to more than 40,000 runners—from the world's best to complete novices—who will start, discover, battle, and ultimately finish something they once thought impossible, even ridiculous: the Chicago Marathon, a daunting distance of 26 miles, 385 yards.

Today's Chicago Marathon route is an unparalleled city showcase, passing Millennium Park, the Loop, Lincoln Park Zoo, Lake Shore Drive, the Lyric Opera House, the Mercantile Exchange, Greek Town, Chinatown, the White Sox ballpark, Sears Tower, and finally, the Grant Park finish area.

It's a spectacular journey, but not one without its challenges. There is a point for every runner on marathon Sunday when, in the face of increasing fatigue, aches, pain and the devilishly tempting opportunity to simply stop, they will choose to continue. Why?

Because the runners are there for a reason: to fulfill a once-in-a-lifetime goal; to run a personal best; to disprove those who say they can't; or simply to do something once seemed beyond reach.

And as they approach the finish line, these reasons make Chicago's marathoners proud heroes to a Chicago that values achievement, to the appreciative charities that the runners support, to their admiring families and children, and yes, somewhere deep inside, to themselves. Remember this was once inconceivable.

There is no better place to view the entire human emotional spectrum than at the finish line. There you will see elation, exhaustion, exhilaration, frustration, pain, relief, hugs of excitement, and tears of joy.

More important, you will see the everyday heroes who capture the never-give-up spirit of Chicago, the same spirit that led to the founding of the Chicago Marathon.

This book takes the reader into their marathon experience, the sights, landscapes, emotions, challenges, and achievements. This book is written and designed specifically for runners who want to know what it's really like to be inside the marathon.

The first chapter, Chicago's First Marathon: 1905, takes the reader through that epic first marathon, the twists, turns, and ultimate crowning of Chicago's first marathon winner.

The second chapter illustrates the heritage and evolution of the marathon's classic era, including marathon heroes, extraordinary efforts, course changes, and the emergence of a world class marathon in Chicago.

The third chapter leaps ahead to the 100th anniversary of the first Chicago Marathon, to explore the modern marathon era. Note that this chapter is not intended to be a chronological highlight reel of all Chicago Marathon winners. Instead it focuses on the dynamics of Chicago racing in its second century.

The fourth chapter combines the past and present into a visual set of parallels, images taken 100 years apart that illustrate the some things never change, even in Chicago marathons.

Next the fifth chapter showcases the Chicago Marathon from start to finish in a guided photograph tour of the course, with advice and commentary designed to help runners navigate the grandest 26.2 miles in the marathon world.

Finally the last chapter focuses on the Chicago Marathon running community, those that make the event so special: the age group runners, the charity teams, the ones who run for fun, and the ones who aim high. Chicago is their race; this book is their experience.

You can live a small lifetime in a marathon. This is what it looks like.

1

CHICAGO'S FIRST

MARATHON

1905

"Chicago's first marathon is to be held this afternoon under the auspices of the new Illinois Athletic Club," announced the feature *Chicago Tribune* article published September 23, 1905. "It is claimed that the field is made up of the best group of men gathered together for a [marathon] in this country, and officials of the Illinois Athletic Club think the Marathon record . . . will be broken."

Among the runners included in the elite field were Sidney Hatch of River Forest (to the right of the tree), a 17-year-old running phenomenon Hatch had previously earned eighth place in the 1904 Olympic Games, held in St. Louis. Small in stature but large in heart and spirit, Hatch delighted spectators and earned loud cheers. In this photograph, the cheers are the last thing on his mind. He has his game face on; he is ready to run.

Albert Corey, right, arrived at the first marathon with strong credentials. A Frenchman-turned-Chicago resident, he ran representing the Chicago Athletic Club. At the 1904 Olympic Games, Corey had won the marathon silver medal. Many are convinced that Corey should have been awarded the gold medal after the revelation that the winner had used performance-enhancing strychnine and alcohol concoctions during the race for the last 18 miles.

Some 20 runners were expected to start; 15 arrived at the Evanston Golf Club, site of the start of the race, shown here, in anticipation of the first running of the Chicago Marathon. The marathon course ran eastward toward Lake Michigan, then southbound along the lake to Grant Park, and then further south to finish in the Washington Park horse-racing track.

Louis Marks, representing the Mohawk Valley Athletic Club of New York, was the race favorite. It was no surprise that Marks sped into the lead position from the start and maintained a healthy lead for many miles. Here Marks has the lead, running through Evanston on Ridge Road, followed by an official race vehicle and bike riders.

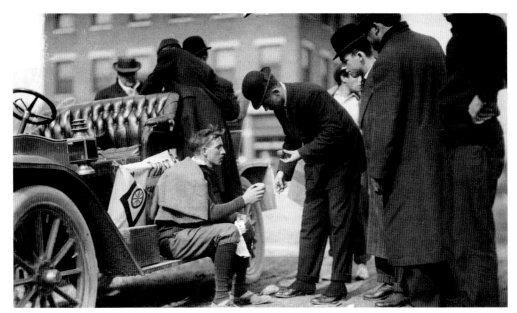

After about five miles, the runners veered right onto southbound Sheridan Road. The surface of the road was dusty, and considerable dust was dispersed into the air by vehicles and bikes, much to the consternation of runners. A few runners paused for lemons and oranges as means of immediate relief from throat irritation before continuing.

In the shadow of race favorite Marks, who was extending his lead, Rhud Metzner of the Illinois Athletic Club ran a balanced, conservative race. Here at the 10-mile point, Metzner is shown running in good form, surrounded by race vehicles and men in suits. Note the crowd beginning to build on both sides of the road.

Race officials knew of potential race interruptions that might impact the outcome. Most notably, the Rush Street Bridge, shown above, was of concern. At 3:25 p.m. Louis Marks, Metzner, and J. J. Kennedy made it across the bridge just as it was turning to allow a steamer through. Other runners did not make it in time and were delayed significantly. It was now a three-man race.

Marks remained in the lead, but not out of sight of Metzner and Kennedy, for the next several miles. In this image, he is still leading, completely surrounded by vehicles and crowds that had continued to grow in size as the race wore on. But he was tiring; as he approached 39th Street, he slowed to a walk. With six miles to go, this was not good.

Seeing Louis Marks in distress, Rhud Metzner suddenly became fresh and energized, steadily speeding up from the rear to take the lead (shown here). Fearing defeat as Metzner moved out of sight, Marks dug deep to respond, catching up to run even with Metzner the next few blocks. But it seemed that only a race delay could allow Marks time to get his energy back.

Almost unbelievably, upon approaching 40th Street, it appeared that the arriving freight train would delay the race. But the train engineer obliged officials and let the runners through. Soon after, with two miles to go, Marks collapsed. Metzner sped onward to enter Washington Park racetrack, above, to screams of 15,000 paying spectators. Metzner took the victory, Kennedy finished second, and Marks was taken to the hospital. The first Chicago Marathon was history.

2

STARTING LINES

CLASSIC ERA

The classic era for Chicago Marathons extended from the first running in 1905 into the early 1920s. The Chicago Marathon as organized by the Illinois Athletic Club was staged annually in late September until 1909. After that, *Chicago Daily News* sponsored Chicago marathons in most years until 1920. Sidney Hatch would ultimately emerge as Chicago's most enduring runner of the classic era. Not only would he finish more than 45 marathons by 1922, he became a record-setting, ultra-distance runner. In October 1916, he ran 96 miles from Milwaukee to Chicago in a record-setting 14 hours, 50 minutes, and 30 seconds.

In 1906, the Chicago Marathon created a new course that would remain the standard for years to come. The new course began at Ravinia Park in Highland Park and ended in Grant Park in front of the Illinois Athletic Building at 112 South Michigan Avenue. This course overlaps the current Chicago Marathon for several North Side miles. In the image above, runners wait for the start of the October 1, 1906, Chicago Marathon outside a stone Ravinia Park building.

This 1906 photograph is a group portrait including Alex Thibeau (right) and Albert Corey (second from right). Thibeau and Corey were expected to contend for victory in the 1906 Chicago Marathon, but Canadian Dennis Bennett took the honors finishing in 2:41:33. Thibeau finished 5th, and Corey was a disappointing 10th. Both would run better in the future.

STARTING LINES: CLASSIC ERA

Thibeau's chance came in the next Chicago Marathon, which resulted in a most extraordinary *Chicago Tribune* headline on September 27, 1907: "Sleeping Runner Loses Marathon; Lindquist Trots Two Miles as Somnambulist; Collapses a Mile from Goal." Today's marathoners know the feeling: the last miles can be staggeringly painful. But it is not sleep; it is delirious exhaustion. William Lindquist, above, overplayed his hand and paid for it in the end.

Lindquist's collapse became Thibeau's gain, as he employed the same steady race strategy that earned Rhud Metzner the Chicago Marathon title years earlier. As a result, it was not a fast race, as Thibeau finished in 3 hours and 10 seconds. Corey ran better in this race, winning second place, more than six minutes behind Thibeau.

Albert Corey's moment came in shortly thereafter, as he took on an ultimate challenge: run 96 miles from Milwaukee to Chicago. In this image, Corey and Sidney Hatch are running on a wide dirt road during the "ultramarathon." The automobile driving on the road behind the runners is carrying timing officials. Hatch is wearing a suit, tie, and hat (no jacket), having joined to pace Corey for a few miles.

Corey finished the solo event with energy to spare. Joined by an unidentified runner and a cyclist in tow, Corey sprints towards the finish line along the city's lakefront, during the final stages of the 96-mile race from Milwaukee to Chicago. Corey set a new record for the distance of slightly more than 16 hours.

Corey continued on to win his first marathon on September 19, 1908. The race boasted the largest field of runners ever. His victory was less than expected however. Despite the 96-mile success, Corey's performances had resulted in loss of sponsors and athletic club affiliation. On this day, Corey rose above and beyond the challenge and won a decisive victory to become the fourth Chicago Marathon champion.

The fifth annual Chicago Marathon again featured the largest group of runners in race history, but the October 2 race proved so challenging that only 31 racers finished. One reason may have been that this was the third marathon run in Chicago in 1909 (the other two were held in January and May). This image shows marathoner William Kessler running along Sheridan Road and Lake Shore Drive in Chicago. He failed to finish the race.

Running behind William Kessler, Peter Kolnis rounds the corner on a dirt road on the course that started in Highland Park. Kolnis was one of several newcomers who were trying to become marathoners. In addition to three marathons in 1909, the heat on this October day became overwhelming, sidelining many runners.

Runners always had medical assistance nearby at all times, and often services were required up and down the racecourse. Not unlike conditions experienced a century later in extreme heat of the 2007 marathon, this was a serious medical situation; vehicles stopped on the road, and spectators and a policeman are visible in the background.

STARTING LINES: CLASSIC ERA

Fighting his way through the heat and other strong runners who remained in good form, James C. Morelan thought he might find his way to snatch victory in the October 1909 Chicago Marathon. Morelan is seen here running on a street in Chicago about three miles from the finish line. Pictured above, evidence of excitement about Morelan's chances is indicated by the multiple automobiles, bicyclists, and spectators around him.

Despite bold challenges by Morelan, and Sydney Hatch, teenager L. J. Pillivant of Hamilton Park came from behind to win the fifth annual Chicago Marathon. By this time, the officially recognized marathon distance was 26 miles, 385 yards, and Pillivant's time was 2:55:15. Observers were stunned. The *Chicago Tribune* headline read: "Boy Outraces 71 in I.A.C. Chicago Marathon." Hatch was again second.

By 1909, the finish area of the Chicago Marathon at the Illinois Athletic Club had become a gathering spot for tens of thousands of spectators. Bands entertained finishers from the balcony, and runners were able to enjoy an after-marathon party. This scene quite resembles the current Chicago Marathon finish area at Columbus Drive and Balbo Avenue.

STARTING LINES: CLASSIC ERA

3

100 Years Later

The Modern Era

The 100th anniversary of the first Chicago Marathon was celebrated on October 9, 2005. Except few, if any, of the runners in the 2005 marathon had any idea of the sort. Most knew only the modern era Chicago Marathons that began in 1977. Progressively through the 1980s, 1990s, and 2000s, the race grew into a first-class event with unmatched elite talent and one of the largest fields of marathon runners in the world.

Since its first running in 1905, Chicago's marathon has inspired hundreds of thousands of people. This banner, placed on the Randolph Street overpass, greets every one of nearly 40,000 runners

who start the Chicago Marathon each year. The message is a theme of Chicago's 2016 Olympic bid, but it applies to all who have run the marathon since 1905.

At 7:20 a.m. on October 9, 2005, bundled-up runners, families, and friends made their way to the starting line of the 2005 Chicago Marathon. Soon they would join more than 35,000 runners and nearly a million spectators who would participate in and witness what was quietly but notably the 100th anniversary of the race.

In Chicago's first marathon in 1905, there were seven finishers. Some 100 years later, 32,995 finishers crossed the line in Grant Park, including those shown above. What a difference a century makes.

In the 1900s, it was significant when the marathon field had grown to over 100 runners. But participant growth in the modern era has been staggering. In 1977, 4,200 runners registered, and 2,128 finished. By 1997, 16,000 runners registered, and by 2005, the race was capped at 40,000 entries, soon to be 45,000 by 2007.

Joan Benoit delivered one of the most memorable Chicago marathon victories in the 1980s. After winning the 1984 Summer Olympics women's marathon with a time of 2:24.52, she came to Chicago to win the 1985 marathon. Her finish time of 2:21:21 was an American record, and it would last for 18 more years. It was eventually broken by Deena Kastor at the London Marathon in 2003.

Khalid Khannouchi has become synonymous with the Chicago Marathon and world-record setting performances. In 1997, he ran his debut marathon in Chicago and won with a time of 2:07:10, which ranked as the fourth fastest marathon time in the world. In 1999, Khalid returned to win in Chicago, this time shattering the world record, reducing it to 2:05:42. He won again in 2000 and 2002 to become the only four-time winner of the Chicago Marathon.

Paula Radcliffe ran the fastest women's marathon in Chicago history. On October 13, 2002, she ran a stunning 2:17:18, breaking the previous world record by 89 seconds. The record she broke had been set a year earlier by Katherine Ndereba of Kenya in the 2001 Chicago Marathon. Radcliffe's extraordinary 2002 race may remain the fastest ever run in the city.

Deena Kastor came to Chicago in 2005 with an impressive resume including the 2004 Olympic bronze medal and the American marathon record. It was her time to win Chicago. In a bold move, Kastor snagged the lead after 5 kilometers (about 3 miles), and stayed there for the next 23 miles. At the end, Kastor was suffering and in trouble. Defending women's champion Constantina Tomescu-Dita's last minute surge failed, however, and Kastor won by five seconds.

Constantina Tomescu-Dita has become an icon of women's running at the Chicago Marathon in recent years. She won the 2004 marathon in 2:23:45, nearly a minute ahead of her next rival. In her battle with Deena Kastor in 2005, all was not lost. Her second place finish time of 2:21:30 was a world record for women aged 35 and older. She returned in 2008 to take fourth place, just a few weeks after winning the Beijing Olympics marathon gold medal.

Robert Cheruiyot is legendary for winning the big races, including New York and Boston on four occasions. In 2006, he set his sights on adding Chicago to his championships. He ran a great race and approaching the finish, he had a five second lead. But at the finish line, he slipped backwards cracking his head on the pavement. It was ruled his torso broke the finish plane, and he was awarded the victory with a time of 2:07:35.

Berhane Adere burst into the Chicago Marathon record books with a surprise win against Galine Bogomolova that went down to the wire in 2006. Adere was able to outsprint Bogolomova and win by five seconds in 2:20:42. Her attempt to defend the championship in 2007 seemed doomed until she achieved the most surprising comeback in Chicago history to win in 2:33:49.

Adriana Pirtea came to Chicago for her marathon debut in 2007. Despite a searing weather forecast, she told her coach "I feel great!" just before the race began. And she did, nearly running away with the race. Pirtea led by 30 seconds on approach to the finish but began celebrating early. Adere took advantage of this mistake and sprinted past a stunned Pirtea to snatch the win.

CHICAGO MARATHON

The 2007 Chicago Marathon featured what might have been the best field of elite male runners in the race's history. In the image above, Felix Limo, 2005 winner (far right); Robert Cheruiyot, 2006 champion (left-center); and Daniel Njenga, consistent top-three finisher (background, left of Cheruiyot) begin prerace warm-up. Seen below, walking back to the starting line, Evans Rutto, 2003 and 2004 champion (far left), joins the group. Before the race (run in record-breaking heat conditions) was over, Rutto and Limo had dropped out, and Cheruiyot shuffled across the finish line in a disappointing fourth place.

Chicago has featured a wheelchair racing division since 1989, when 19 year-old Scott Hollenbeck of Champaign, Illinois, won the race in 1:45:30. Ann Cody-Morris, also from the Champaign area, took the women's title that year in 1:58:51. Since then, Illinois wheelchair racers have dominated the winner's circle, though Kurt Fearnley of Austria, champion in 2007 and 2008, is trying to change that. These images capture wheelchair racers just after the start of the 2008 race, immediately organizing themselves into drafting formation for better aerodynamics and faster speeds.

The 2007 marathon took place in unseasonably hot conditions. At 7:30 a.m., air temperatures approached 80 degrees, and there was significant reason for concern. Runners tend to suffer in excessive heat conditions, becoming especially vulnerable to dehydration. These images show the start of the race at 8:00 a.m., when some were already beginning to overheat. As the sun rose and conditions worsened, aid stations ran out of water and some athletes began collapsing from heat stroke. In response to preserve runner safety, organizers chose to suspend the race after three and a half hours had elapsed. Nearly 11,000 runners were directed to leave the course and return to Grant Park. Despite the frustration of those who were not able to complete their race, many were convinced the race director Carey Pinkowski's courageous decision ultimately saved lives.

Chicago has always been a co-ed race, with the mix of women runners hovering around 40 percent in recent years. In 2005, 14,322 women finished the marathon, among 32,995 overall finishers. In 2008, those numbers subsided somewhat, as 13,688 women completed the race out of 31,343 total finishers. As noted earlier, the field of elite runners has been equally impressive in both the men's and women's divisions. The elite women's field in the 2008 race, shown above, included former champions Constantina Tomescu-Dita, Berhane Adere, Adere's 2007 rival Adriana Pirtea, and recent Boston marathon winner Lidiya Grigoryeva. Top runners from the men's elite field, Emmanual Mutai, Evans Cheruiyot, and David Mandago, are shown below taking the lead in the 2008 race.

This image of the 2008 elite women runners illustrates dynamics at the start of a race. Elite women and men start at the same time, but the men's pack quickly outpaces the women. The elite women are then left to work together in the beginning to find a pace that is challenging but not taxing. Here Adriana Pirtea can be seen, rear center, just in front of Berhane Adere. For the next 14 miles, this group stayed together, matching each other stride for stride.

Similar dynamics are the norm in the men's race, with an added attraction. Race organizers routinely pay runners—called "Pacers"—to lead the elite men to the 13.1-mile point at an agreed-upon pace. Interestingly this practice is similar to the pacer concept employed in 1905 and onward where each runner was accompanied by a vehicle, bicyclists, and other runners helping set the pace. In this image, the lead two pacers have been instructed to take the elite runners to the halfway point in just under one hour and three minutes. After that, their job is done, and the men's race usually breaks wide open.

CHICAGO MARATHON

These images capture the lead women at the 13.1-mile point in the 2008 race. Note that the women, without benefit of a contracted pacer, have remained in tight formation the entire first part of the race. Several runners in this group have the ability to win, including Colleen DeReuck (far left), Adere Berhane, and Lidiya Grigoryeva. The question is who will make the first move.

Just past 13.1 miles, the elite men run toward the West Loop in a small subset of the original pack. The group in this image have fallen behind the leaders soon after the pacers finished their work. The gap between this quartet and the leaders has grown quickly and mercilessly. None of these runners have a chance of winning now.

100 YEARS LATER: MODERN ERA

Evans Cheruiyot and David Mandago continued to run side-by-side until the 40k mark, when Cheruiyot had achieved a 17-second lead. After that, he never looked back. It was only the second marathon of his career, and Evans Cheruiyot won the 2008 Chicago Marathon in a time of 2:06:25. Mandago would ultimately finish more than a minute later, in 2:07:37. A race champion is allowed little time to rest and shortly after accepting congratulations from executive race director Carey Pinkowski (white hat, below), Cheruiyot was consumed by the media. It was easy for him to smile; his victory was worth $100,000.

CHICAGO MARATHON

In the women's race, the pack had shattered by mile 15. Lidiya Grigoryeva and Alevtina Biktirmirova shot into the lead, running 5:25 miles to break the contest into a two-woman race. Grigoryeva, the better 10k runner of the two, had the upper hand, and she used it. She sprinted ahead of Biktirmirova to a lead of nearly two minutes by mile 21. A gap of that size, that deep into a race, is rarely closed unless the leader has made serious mistakes along the way. Grigoryeva had run a perfect race and held on to win easily in 2:27:17. Here she is, just after crossing the line, thrilled with the victory.

100 YEARS LATER: MODERN ERA

Constantina Tomescu-Dita, a consistently strong marathoner and former Chicago Marathon champion, had won the 2008 Olympic marathon gold medal just 57 days earlier. Winning the gold was exceptional; she became the oldest Olympic marathon champion at age 38. That would have been enough for most runners, but Tomescu-Dita wanted to return to Chicago. Few expected her to contest for the win, but she delivered a solid fourth place finish in 2:30:19. When she finished, shown above, her smile and demeanor were assuredly relaxed, as if she had just completed an easy jog.

Their 2008 marathons over, new champion Lidiya Grigoryeva (center top) and former champion Constantina Tomescu-Dita (lower center) get a well-deserved escort from the finish line to the post-race press conference. There's nothing better than a breezy walk after running the race of a lifetime.

100 YEARS LATER: MODERN ERA

4

PARALLELS

THEN AND NOW

A century between Chicago's classic- and modern-era marathons might not be all that different in certain ways. The most obvious of these similarities is what the experience looks and feels like at various points in the race. The visual parallels can be timeless, and some things never change. On June 30, 1913, runners are poised to start a Chicago Daily News–sponsored race, shown above. The starting line on a wide dirt track in Grant Park is approximately the same spot where today's Chicago Marathons begin. In the background are Michigan Avenue buildings, and the Art Institute of Chicago stands behind the runners. In 2008, tens of thousands of runners would be standing in that exact spot, in parallel, as then became now.

A century years later, in roughly the same spot as the photograph on the previous page, nearly 40,000 runners are closely packed shoulder-to-shoulder on Columbus Avenue at the start of the 2008 Chicago Marathon. This image only captures the first few thousand runners. The mass of

runners continues south on Columbus for nearly half a mile. In a crowd this big, runners have to be patient. It takes several minutes for the last runner to cross the starting line.

In 1905 and subsequent classic-era Chicago Marathon races, each runner was assigned an official trailing car containing a race official, a medical doctor, and two running pacers. The idea to have a race official accompany each runner by car emerged after substantial fraud had occurred in the 1904 Olympic marathon in St. Louis. In that race, Thomas Hicks began ingesting performance enhancing combinations of strychnine and alcohol beginning at mile 11. He won the gold medal, but it was a tainted victory. A century later, the only vehicles in the Chicago Marathon are television and press vehicles. In the image below, elite runners begin the 2008 marathon under the watchful cameras on motorcycles and trucks that will ride ahead, recording every move, nod, and wink for the entire 26.2 miles.

PARALLELS: THEN AND NOW

Several pace vehicles are aligned together, waiting for the start of the 2008 Marathon. After the race begins, the vehicles split up to cover wheelchair, men's, and women's races independently.

In the first Chicago Marathons, the number of starters was so few that it seemed rare to find runners running in packs for very long. The runners usually were determined to run their own race, alone. This rare image captures three of Chicago's most prominent marathoners at the time—Alex Thibeau, Albert Corey and Sidney Hatch—with two others, running together in the 1907 Chicago Marathon. They ran together for many miles on an unpaved Sheridan Road with Lake Michigan immediately to their left. In today's marathons, group running is the norm for elite racers for the first 13.1 miles. The image below of the entire 2008 women's elite field is representative of early-race strategy and tactics: stay close, stay steady, prepare to make a decisive move in the second half of the race. After that, may the best runner win.

PARALLELS: THEN AND NOW

In 1909, L. J. Pillivant stunned the marathon community as a teenager winning the Chicago Marathon against more experienced runners. Above, Pillivant finds himself boxed in on all sides by motor vehicles, bicycles, and race officials. In 2008, the same scene played out in the women's race, shown below. Here, approaching 13.1 miles into the marathon, the women are surrounded by a complement including an official timing car and various media and security motorcycles at the side and the rear.

Here is something not seen every day, whether it be 1908 or 2008: runners taking to the sidewalk in a marathon. In the image above, the runners had left the street in an attempt to avoid significant dust that was kicked up by accompanying cars, bicycles, and even horses and buggies. The dust caused severe throat and allergy problems for some runners, so the sidewalk became part of the solution. For similar reasons, Albert Corey took to the sidewalk to win his first Chicago Marathon in 1908. A century later, the two runners below were wishing that getting onto the sidewalk would ease their suffering. It was 2007, and the runners were 700 meters from the finish line, struggling mightily against heat exhaustion. The race had been officially canceled just minutes earlier, but these runners pushed on through the pain to cross the finish line. They were among the last finishers on that heat-shortened marathon day.

There is something truly special in seeing the lead runner emerge in the distance, slowly approaching the finish line on his way to victory after 26.2 long and grueling miles. In 1908, above, it was Albert Corey running down a dirt road toward his hard-earned Chicago Marathon victory. In 2008, below, it was Evans Cheruiyot turning the corner from Roosevelt Drive onto Columbus Drive for the final 0.2 miles of his marathon. In the moments when one sees the eventual victor moving closer, the spirit of his success and the thrill of his impending victory can be felt throughout the cheering crowd.

And finally, it is over. The champion has run the course, outsmarted the opponents, made the right moves, salvaged the bad decisions, and has put it all together for one very extraordinary right: to raise his arms in salute to his victory and to the city that has welcomed him to the line. In an image similar to marathon runner Alfred A. Schwiderski nearing the finish in 1909, above. Below, Lidiya Grigoryeva runs between two officials to break the finish line tape, sealing her 2008 Chicago Marathon victory.

PARALLELS: THEN AND NOW

5

THE JOURNEY

26.2 MILES

The point of the journey is not just to finish; it is to get the most out of the experience. This is what Chicago's marathon looks like from the runner's perspective, from start to finish, the entire 26.2-mile race.

Before race day, there is some business to attend to. Once runners are registered for the race, it is then time to enjoy the prerace exposition; it is the appetizer to the event. There is an incredible buzz of excitement as thousands of runners pick up their race numbers, all of them anticipating a great day. Runners can walk every aisle, sample different items, talk to exhibitors and other runners, and soak it all in.

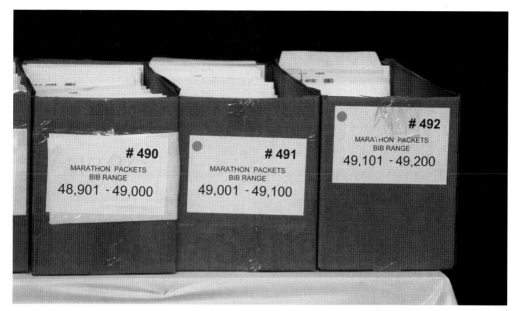

At the exposition, runners pick up their bib numbers and timing chips. The number is the ticket into the starting area and a permission slip to run the marathon. That box on the upper right indicates that there are bib numbers as high as 49,200 in the race. Numbers are colorized in such a way to indicate each runner's starting group. The number 6,266 puts one runner in the "competitive" staging area; the person picking up the 49,200 bib number will, theoretically, start at the back of an extremely long line.

It helps to know where one is going on race day. This couple studies the course map at the race exposition. Chicago's marathon course delivers an experience that rivals any major marathon in the world. It is an unparalleled city showcase of the best Chicago has to offer, including distinctive neighborhoods, enthusiastic spectators, and the spirit of community throughout the entire city.

When 40,000 runners begin to move toward the starting line on Grant Park, things will slow down fast. Marathon organizers do a nice job of directing traffic and getting runners in the right starting areas (designated by bib color and number), but the process may take much longer than one thinks. Assuming that runners are waiting in a warm spot nearby, they should move toward the starting line no later than 6:30 a.m.

As the clock ticks closer to the 8:00 a.m. start time, runners look around. They smile and greet others nearby. They ask where others are from and what kind of day they are expecting on the course. They pat one another on the back and wish one another luck. It is good karma and part of sharing the experience with the running community.

Before runners know it, the starting gun will fire, and the race will begin. However, that may not be true for a runner who is near the end of the pack of 40,000 participants. For those at the back, the clock will pass 8:00 a.m., and they might not move for a while. That is the nature of pushing tens of thousands of people down a six-lane road all at once.

This is when the fun begins. With Millenium Park on the left, runners will travel under the Randolph Street Overpass, which will be lined with screaming spectators and a few television cameras. They can look up, smile, and wave. Then runners disappear on lower Columbus Avenue for about a quarter mile heading toward the Chicago River. The runners will know what to do when they get to this tunnel-like area: whoop it up. Everyone around will be doing it, and it is just one of the early parts of a race experience runners will never forget.

Runners then get into a steady groove and enjoy, for lack of a better word, the first 13 miles that will travel through Lincoln Park, Wrigleyville, Old Town, River North, and the Loop. The runners should feel good, and if they have been training enough, it will feel relatively easy.

After heading north for the first several hundred meters, the course does a U-turn, taking runners southbound across the State Street bridge, toward the two-mile marker at Jackson Street.

THE JOURNEY: 26.2 MILES

On the way to Jackson Street, runners pass the Marina Towers (above) and travel through the city's theater district. At this point, runners will be approaching the first water and Gatorade station. They should grab a cup and try to sip while running or slow to a walk. There is no hurry, as there will be water stations every mile. To each person who hands out a cup, runners should say, "Thank you for being here."

The first couple of miles have been an easy warm-up for most runners. That begins to change after the turn from Jackson Street onto LaSalle Street, running north through the corridor of Chicago's financial center. If participants want to start running faster, this is the place to do it.

THE JOURNEY: 26.2 MILES

Participants then run south on LaSalle Street for nearly two miles to reach the Lincoln Park Zoo. During those two miles, runners should be taking inventory of their running form and condition. They should ask themselves if things are going well or if it seems harder than expected. They should consider if their legs feel stiff or strong and if their breathing is labored or steady. Paying attention to these things will make a difference in the race.

Before runners know it, they have reached the five-mile marker in the center of Lincoln Park Zoo. In this particular image, the race timing clock is obscured by the mile marker. That is not a bad thing; it is too early to begin worrying about time. Runners should run at the pace that feels right. Below is the Lincoln Park Conservatory, which was a featured landmark in the classic-era Chicago Marathons of 1905 and on. Participants are now running through history, following in the footstep of true Chicago running pioneers.

THE JOURNEY: 26.2 MILES

The miles start flying by. The timing clock at the six-mile marker says 52 minutes have expired. This means the pace is about 8 minutes 40 seconds per mile. It is an easy pace, on track to arrive around a four-hour finish time. Not great news for the runner at the bottom center; she is aiming to run a 3:30 marathon time. The course continues north on Sheridan Road and then Lake Shore Drive to Addison Street. Again participants are running on historic ground. Next is the turn from Addison Street onto Broadway Street, seen below. Time to return to the Loop.

Shortly after the turn onto north Broadway Street, there is another time check. Then runners pass the eight-mile and nine-mile points. This is when they begin giving themselves credit for completing more than one-third of the course, almost. Runners want to feel steady and strong at this point.

A wooded neighborhood on Sedgwick Street, above, approaching Old Town is a very pleasant break from the big city sights. The relative peace lasts long enough for runners to pass the 10-mile point, and then it is time for something different, seen below. Elvis is alive and well, entertaining runners on Division Street.

Entertainment may be more than necessary with the 11-mile checkpoint just ahead. Things can start to feel tough here. At this point, runners are not even halfway done. Runners must stay strong and focus on their trip back into the Loop.

THE JOURNEY: 26.2 MILES

As runners make their way southbound on Wells Street, east on Hubbard Street, and south again on Orleans Street, they will start to hear the growing roar of the crowd deep in the Loop. These cheers help pull runners toward the Loop for miles 9 to 12. As they pass the Merchandise Mart, below, they pay no attention to the Do Not Enter traffic signal.

The course takes runners south on Franklin Street into the Loop. At this point, runners have reached the 20-kilometer mark, almost halfway to the end. The increasing noise is located at the corner of Franklin and Adams Streets, seen below.

THE JOURNEY: 26.2 MILES

When runners turn onto westbound Adams Street approaching their 13th mile, they will feel like they are in the middle of a parade. Thousands of spectators will be cheering for them. It is a great spectacle. Runners should soak it in and enjoy it, because the course may begin to push back soon.

Then it gets different. When heading west to mile 14 on Adams Street, things thin out a lot. It still helps to have energized spectators cheering, however. Runners are now heading away from Chicago and still have about halfway to go.

THE JOURNEY: 26.2 MILES

This is 14 miles; this is after two hours of running and probably two hours more before finishing. It is when runners' legs are wearing down and when they should let their mental training take over. The long training runs, common to many when training for a marathon, were not just for their bodies; they also prepared the runners to have the will and the spirit to take it to the extra mile. On race day, runners draw on those training experiences to keep moving, keep steady, and keep themselves in the game.

Participants can break things up by looking forward to passing more of Chicago's distinctive neighborhoods such as Little Italy at mile 17, Pilsen at mile 19, and Chinatown after mile 21.

The view of the city is wonderful while running south on Halsted Street at mile 17, but runners may not feel that way. In many ways they are at the hardest point. They have been strong enough to have made it through two-thirds of the course but still have a very long nine miles to go.

It is more important than ever at this point to hydrate well. Runners should not overdrink, but if they need it, they should make sure to get a cup of energy drink or water at each aid station, like the one seen above in Little Italy on Taylor Street. Runners should also thank the volunteers every time.

And at this point in the race, thoughts will come to runners that they may retain for years. What may seem like an ordinary left turn from Taylor Street onto south Ashland Avenue at mile 18 might be their most lasting memory of this event. It may be the time at which runners discover renewed strength to keep them moving forward.

Approaching Pilsen and mile 19, runners continue to draw energy from the people around them. By now, they may actually recognize runners who have been with/near them for miles. They might talk and have fun with them. The men on the crane in the image above are taking pictures. Runners will note that they have run 30k, about 18.3 miles, in 2 hours, 45 minutes and wonder if they can get to the finish in 4 hours. Doing mental math at this point in the race gets hard, but it is a good distraction.

Runners may get sore by this time, in more places than one. If they run long enough, they will likely get to the point where, as one runner has said, "everything hurts louder than everything else." They must just deal with it, and keep moving forward.

Crossing the Morgan Street bridge on the way to the 20th mile, these runners are with the group aiming for a 3:45 target finishing time. They might wonder if they are running faster than they think, or if they are too slow to meet their goal.

THE JOURNEY: 26.2 MILES

Before Chinatown, participants will run what seems like the longest mile of the day, from Halsted Street to Archer Avenue to Cermak Road. The good news is that there are only five miles to go.

There are many things for runners to look forward to in Chinatown at mile 21. Crowds fill up again, and there is a giant dragon and a television camera or two. When runners make that right turn through Chinatown, they should prepare to smile for the camera.

Runners take a moment to appreciate the surroundings and elaborate decorations. Chinatown is really a special place and an ideal destination on the Chicago Marathon course.

If friends and family want to come support runners, it helps participants to have a rough idea when they might see them. Even if the spectators are not family, it is nice to hear them cheer just the same.

The next thing to look forward to on the trip south is passing by White Sox Park. Runners can look forward to the rock band playing in the shade of the ballpark by the water station. If they wish, participants can walk through this station, drink two cups of Gatorade, momentarily enjoy the music, and then move on. There are approximately four miles to go.

The next three miles can be very difficult. These miles are geographically significant; close enough to downtown, still too far from the finish. But this situation is alleviated by one thought: it will be over soon.

THE JOURNEY: 26.2 MILES

As each step gets harder at this portion of the marathon, simple distractions are welcome. There are the camera guys again. Runners can have their photograph taken, watch others get excited about it, and take a second to see other runners mugging for the camera. Hopefully this will put a little pep in their step, because they will need it.

This is the 24-mile point. This is the beginning of the end. Runners may not really care about their finish time anymore; they just want to know when it is over. On a good day, running the next 2.2 miles can take less than 20 minutes. If runners are feeling less than optimal at this point of the marathon, however, they might be 25 minutes from home. Still, this is great news, as 25 minutes can seem like nothing compared to what they have completed. Those long miles are behind them, and the finish line gets closer with each step.

THE JOURNEY: 26.2 MILES

And as runners get closer, a great landmark will get bigger. The Sears Tower becomes a beacon; each step closer to it is a step closer to their personal victory. Each runner is almost a marathon finisher.

Runners can start enjoying the marathon completely when they reach the corner of Michigan Avenue and Roosevelt Road. There they will turn left to run slightly uphill toward Columbus Avenue. This is the steepest climb of the day, but they are almost done with their marathon.

THE JOURNEY: 26.2 MILES

Runners savor the final turn onto Columbus Drive. There the road opens amazingly wide. After all those miles where runners were so close to one another, all of a sudden they are out in the open, seemingly alone. And they can see the finish line a few hundred yards ahead. This is just like it was in the early 1900s when Rhud Metzner, Dennis Bennett, Albert Corey, Sydney Hatch, L. J. Pillivant, and others finished their Chicago Marathons very near the same finish line location just ahead.

It can be the most wonderful sight, and one that runners will never forget it. At that moment, runners can run straight ahead; they can veer over to the side and high-five spectators; they can look for families and friends who might be there. They just need to be sure to make it across the line.

THE JOURNEY: 26.2 MILES

The elites will cross the finish line starting at about 10:06 a.m. As the runners approach the finish line to end the 2006 Chicago Marathon, the clock is ticking right as they might have expected. It reads 3:59:49, then 3:59:50. And then it is done.

Running a marathon is one of those things many people consider impossible. These runners have overcome the challenge: they have finished the race.

THE JOURNEY: 26.2 MILES

Suddenly runners realize that it is over. What next? First they must keep moving away from the finish area, because roughly four people are crossing the line each second during peak times. Then they might look for their families and friends. It is a fantastic welcome after a great race experience each year.

Runners can learn more about themselves in 26.2 miles than some people have in years. There will be moments when they do not feel well, and there will be moments they feel elated. There

THE JOURNEY: 26.2 MILES

will be moments runners realize that they have gotten through something they never thought they could get through, and those are the best moments of all.

This is a finish medal, something well earned by every runner who receives it. No one can ever take away this accomplishment.

After the greetings and medals, it is time for the runners to rest and relax. Spotters like the ones in this image are on hand to guide finishers to food, drink, family, and friends.

These finishers are now a part of history, following in the footsteps of Chicago's marathon pioneers.

THE JOURNEY: 26.2 MILES

6

SPIRIT OF CHICAGO

THE PEOPLE'S MARATHON

When the Chicago Marathon was revived in 1977, organizers had a vision that it would be the "People's Marathon." And indeed it has been all about the people. 450,000 runners have finished the race since 1905; 45,000 register to participate and 1.5 million spectators watch the race from Chicago's streets each year.

More than 10,000 people volunteer for a wide variety of race day assignments. From handling logistics in the starting area, above, to handing out water or energy drinks at 1 of 20 aid stations on the course to catering to runners at the finish area, below, the volunteers are true champions of the marathon.

The race suffered from serious problems in 2007, when extreme weather conditions led to aid stations running out of water much earlier than anyone ever expected. To ensure that the situation never repeats, in 2008, 100,000 gallons of water and energy drink were distributed among the 20 course aid stations and at the finish line.

More than 700 medical personnel volunteer their services at the finish line to aid runners who may be in need of treatment. In a typical race, issues treated are most often dehydration, exhaustion, and a variety of foot ailments. If help is needed at the end of a race, the team is superb.

Team McGraw raises awareness and research dollars for the quality of life issues that surround a patient and family following a brain tumor diagnosis. Jenny McDevitt, above, is a Team McGraw member who has completed an impressive six Chicago Marathons, one for each year since her brain tumor diagnosis.

A Leukemia and Lymphoma charity runner collapses at the finish, and is helped immediately by volunteers.

Moving scenes of determination and spirit abound at the finish line. This runner fell and appeared completely unable to make it the final few feet to cross the finish line. But he still had fight in him, and he gave it everything he had. He was lifted up by a fellow runner, but the runner stumbled again.

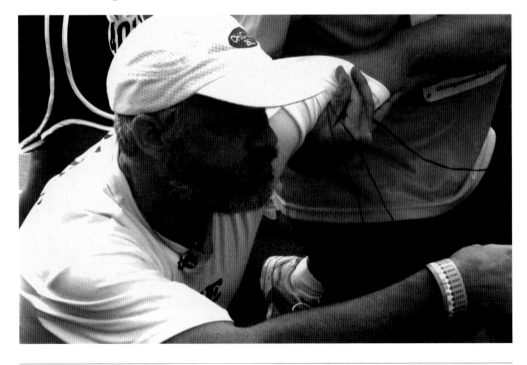

SPIRIT OF CHICAGO: THE PEOPLE'S MARATHON

On his third attempt, the determined runner finally fell across the finish line to complete what would become his ultimate achievement, Chicago's marathon. It was an unbelievable demonstration of the fighting spirit that recalled the vintage days of the first Chicago marathons.

CHICAGO MARATHON

Chicago has been giving back to the community for many years. In 2002, the first year the marathon started tracking fund-raising efforts, 14 teams with 1,674 members raised a combined $3 million com for their charities. In 2008, the Leukemia and Lymphoma Society delivered 706 runners, raising $2.5 million for their cause.

Chicago has had a pace team program for many years. In 2008, more than 100 leaders served as pacers, helping runners to meet certain goal times. For instance, if a runner hoped to finish the marathon in 3 hours and 30 minutes, as in the image above, they would find the group leader for that pace. The leader is usually easy to spot, with the large sign. All a runner has to do is try to stay near the leader for the whole race, and they can meet their goal.

Team World Vision brought 724 runners to the 2008 marathon, raising about $900 per runner, on average. The team members were easily recognized with bright orange jerseys. Some members ran as a group in an additional commitment to team spirit.

This pair cannot believe they have done it. Thousands of runners complete their first marathon in Chicago each year.

The largest percent of female runners comes from the 25–29 age group, representing 11 percent of the field. The 30–34 and 35–39 age groups account for an additional 8 percent and 7 percent, respectively. Less than 1 percent of Chicago's women runners are more than 55 years old.

Every runner has a reason for being out there on the course, for being driven to completing the marathon. This woman dedicated her race to her father. There are many such tributes carried over the course each year.

These women ran the marathon for the thrill of the achievement.

These women are delighted to have finished their first marathons. They once thought it was impossible. They proved otherwise.

Another first-time finisher advertises her goal on her running jersey. She also notes that it is not an easy endeavor; she is also battling shin splints.

Male runners at Chicago tend to be older; 10 percent come from the 35–39 age group. The 30–34 and 25–29 age groups come next, with 9 percent and 8 percent respectively. More than 4 percent of male runners are over 55. The young runner to the left has just jumped onto the road to share the excitement of his father's finish.

This runner dedicated her race to Olivia, a good friend.

The world's press and broadcast media flock to cover the marathon. In 2008, 450 media representatives covered the race. The prime spot is on the press truck, shown here. Hitching a ride is Ryan Hall, bottom right, who represented the U.S. in the 2008 Beijing Olympic marathon.

The marathon charity program has expanded significantly in the last six years. In 2008, 110 charity teams brought 6,745 runners to the marathon, and the contributions earned for their efforts exceeded $10.5 million. The marathoner above, center, is running for Ronald McDonald House Charities.

More than 100 countries and all 50 U.S. states are represented in the marathon. Roughly 55 percent of the 2008 marathoners came from locations other than Illinois.

This trio from Chile had much to celebrate after finishing with better times than they expected. The long flight home would be a happy one.

Mexico was well represented by 1,209 runners in 2008. This number is a dramatic five-fold gain from the 271 athletes who participated in the 1999 race.

SPIRIT OF CHICAGO: THE PEOPLE'S MARATHON

The number of registrants has grown more than 1,000 percent since 1977, when 4,200 signed up to race the first Chicago marathon in more than 50 years.

The 2009 race, limited to 45,000 registrations, sold out in late April, several months before the October race date. Not long ago, a runner could show up the day before the race and sign up.

CHICAGO MARATHON

American Cancer Society was the largest charity team in the 2008 marathon, represented by 811 runners who raised $1.5 million.

Every runner has his or her own personal approach to managing challenges on the course. This runner was not leaving anything to chance, carrying her own water supply in her backpack.

It is amazing how happy some runners can look after a difficult 26.2-mile run. The finish line can have this effect on many participants.

This runner deserves to celebrate. She is finishing the 2005 Chicago Marathon, on the 100th anniversary of Chicago's first marathon. She is part of a history far more epic than she realizes.

A final look back to where running pioneers ran the first Chicago Marathon more than 100 years ago, the finish line in Grant Park.

ABOUT THE AUTHOR

Raymond Britt is managing partner of WinSight Ventures and publisher of RunTri.com. His first race was the 1994 Chicago Marathon, and since then, he has finished 95 marathons and ironman triathlons, earning a U.S.A. Triathlon All-American national ranking. He lives with his wife and four children in the northern suburbs of Chicago.

RunTri.com is a non-profit site dedicated to providing endurance athletes with practical advice and information about training for and racing in major marathons and triathlons. RunTri.com is proud to be of service to 400,000 athletes annually.

Across America, People are Discovering Something Wonderful. Their Heritage.

Arcadia Publishing is the leading local history publisher in the United States. With more than 3,000 titles in print and hundreds of new titles released every year, Arcadia has extensive specialized experience chronicling the history of communities and celebrating America's hidden stories, bringing to life the people, places, and events from the past. To discover the history of other communities across the nation, please visit:

www.arcadiapublishing.com

Customized search tools allow you to find regional history books about the town where you grew up, the cities where your friends and family live, the town where your parents met, or even that retirement spot you've been dreaming about.